Under the Covers

Being in a dream state of mystification. A woman recieves messages from an unknown spirit. To be shared with the collective whos hearts might be touched by this unusual vision of voice.

NANCY E. WYLIE

ARCHWAY
PUBLISHING

Archway Publishing books may be ordered through booksellers or by contacting:

Archway Publishing
1663 Liberty Drive
Bloomington, IN 47403
www.archwaypublishing.com
844-669-3957

Because of the dynamic nature of the Internet, any web addresses or links contained in this book may have changed since publication and may no longer be valid. The views expressed in this work are solely those of the author and do not necessarily reflect the views of the publisher, and the publisher hereby disclaims any responsibility for them.

All images depicted are created and provided by Nancy E. Wylie and are being used for Illustration purposes only.

ISBN: 978-1-6657-2810-2 (sc)
ISBN: 978-1-6657-2809-6 (hc)
ISBN: 978-1-6657-2811-9 (e)

Library of Congress Control Number: 2022914244

Print information available on the last page.

Archway Publishing rev. date: 10/10/2022

Messages from an unknown spirit to be shared with those whose heart shall be touched or felt by this vision of voice.

Unspoken words grow more beautiful when they are spoken. Only then can their true voices be revealed.

We are never really alone or forgotten.

I humbly dedicate this book to the spirit who makes its presence known with its persistent words and epiphanies during my much-needed moments of rest, when my vital body activities choose to cease from my daily activities. My mind in its own rhythm of openness and slumber. In those moments of seemingly subconscious states, a door seems to open to my mind, as if I'm in some kind of receiving mode and in enters this rapid stream of repetitive messages from a voice that repeats a sequence of words.

My mind is like a web that catches the words that are thrown out by energies at an extremely fast pace. The more I tried to ignore it and push it to the side, the louder and more persistent the voice became. I have found the only way to bring the voice to an end is to physically gain consciousness and tumble to my nightstand and write down the message on a piece of paper, which I now conveniently have placed at my bedside. Only then would the voice dissipate. Every night seems to be like a sequel to the night before. I am not opposed to this spiritual connection that wants to share its words. I find the beauty in the situation—even as difficult and intrusive as it is at times when it tries to dominate and interrupt my much-needed sleep. I have learned how to shut the door and put up a wall and place this voice on the shelf. Not to offend them with this adventure but to protect my own reality so I can rest my mind and body and recharge for my own earthly awareness. So I close the door when I need to. I do have compassion and intrigue for what is beyond me and for the spirit who is overlooking this divine act of intervention and its need to bring its messages to these pages to be released into the winds of abyss. So I humbly write down their words to be shared with those who may find and connect with them.

The name of this book and its illustrations and design were given to me in my moments of relaxation and in a mode of unintentional meditation as a soft-spoken whisper.

Being sensitive to the spirit is such a gift, and I am truly appreciative for the guidance, knowledge, and protection I receive from them.

The flutter of your whispers
pass by me as I sleep.

By N.E.W.

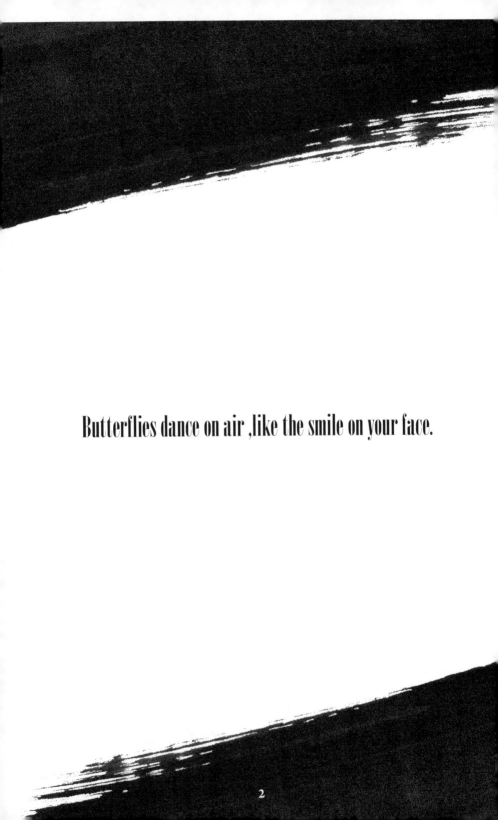

Butterflies dance on air ,like the smile on your face.

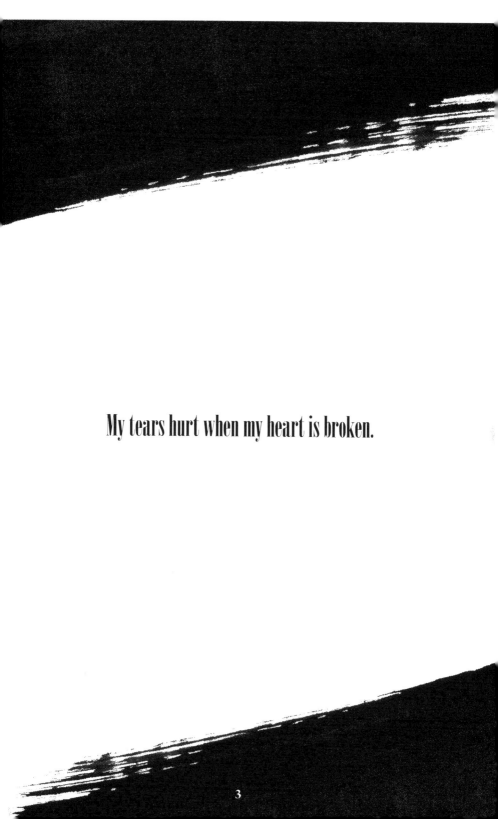

My tears hurt when my heart is broken.

My eyes only see what my soul can feel.

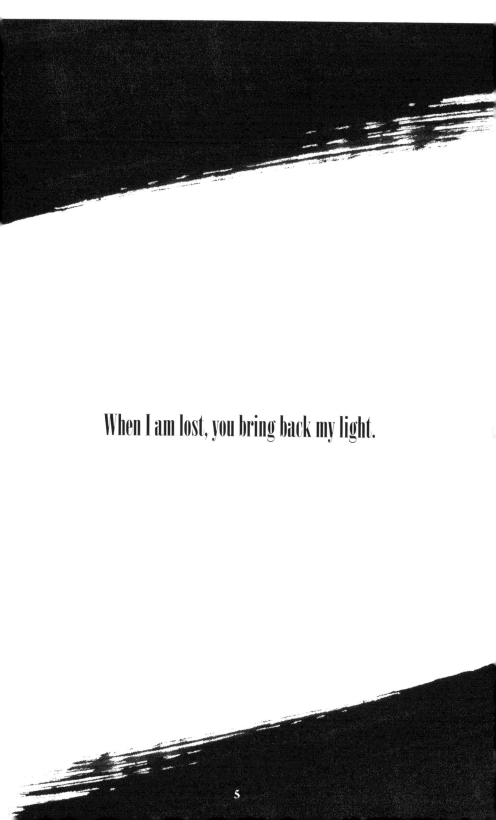

When I am lost, you bring back my light.

My soul cracks when darkness shines.

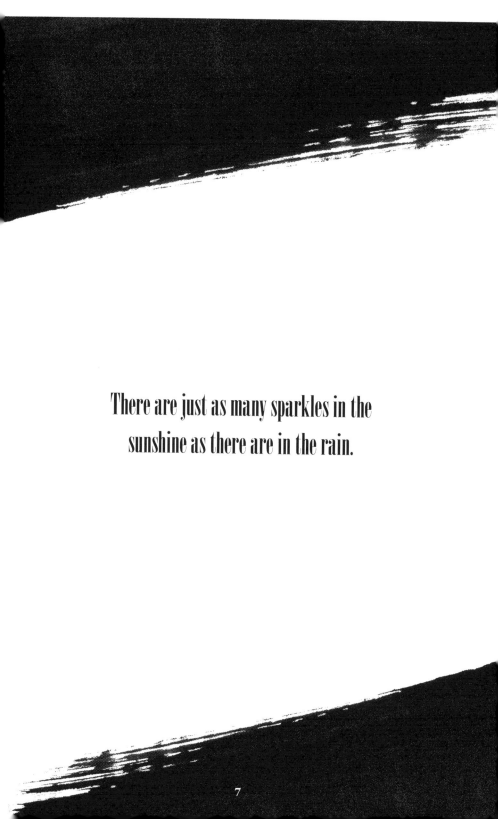

There are just as many sparkles in the
sunshine as there are in the rain.

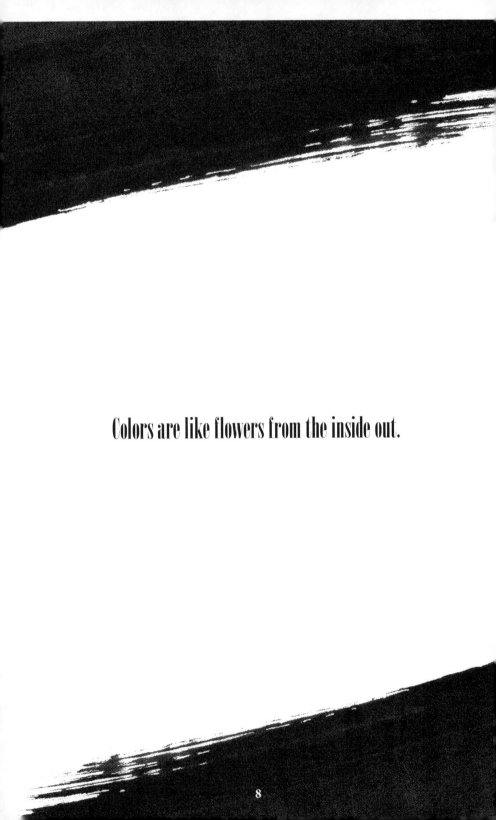

Colors are like flowers from the inside out.

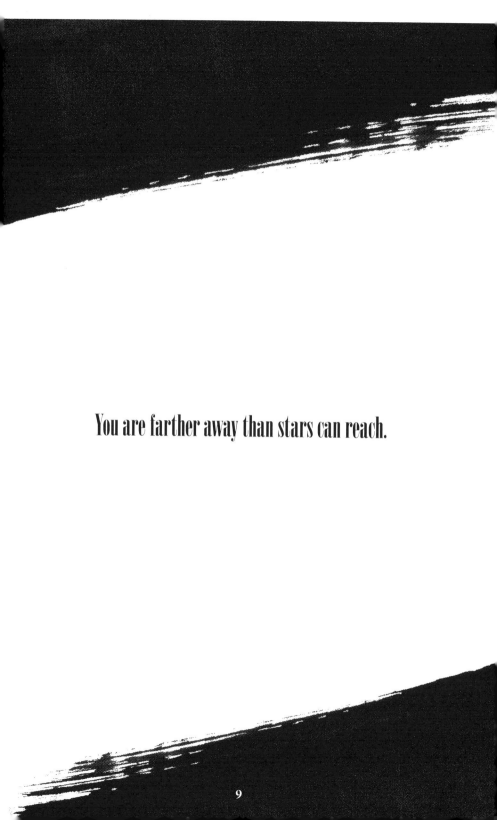

You are farther away than stars can reach.

My eyes are only blue when my soul is gray.

The magic from his fingertips
is like a wand of joy.

By N.E.W.

His countenance is warm with thought.

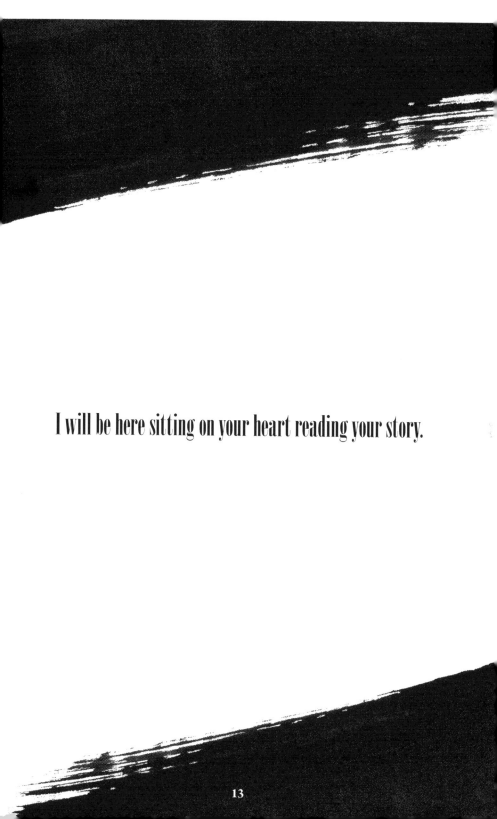

I will be here sitting on your heart reading your story.

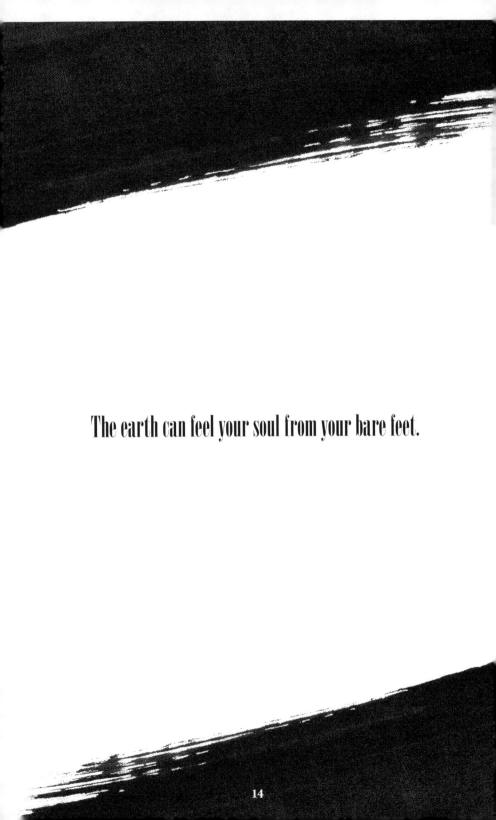

The earth can feel your soul from your bare feet.

Your touch is pure magic when magic is pure.

Fire is only hot when felt.

Flowers bloom when your soul smiles.

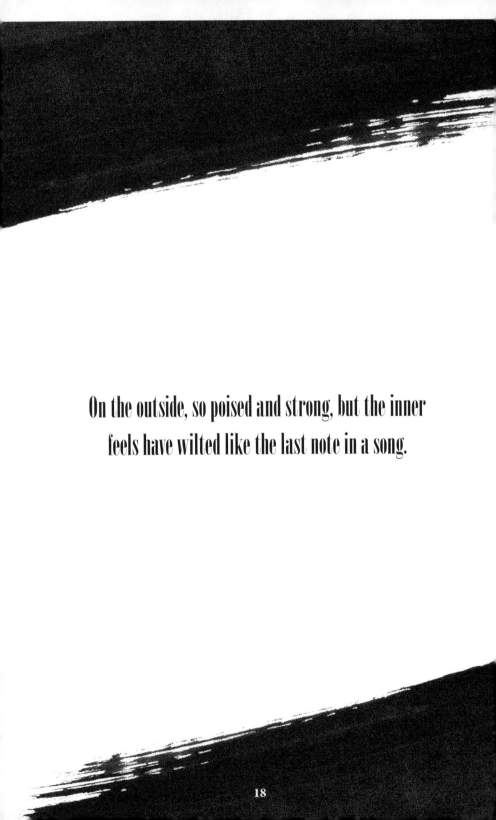

On the outside, so poised and strong, but the inner feels have wilted like the last note in a song.

You gave my smile a soul of her own.

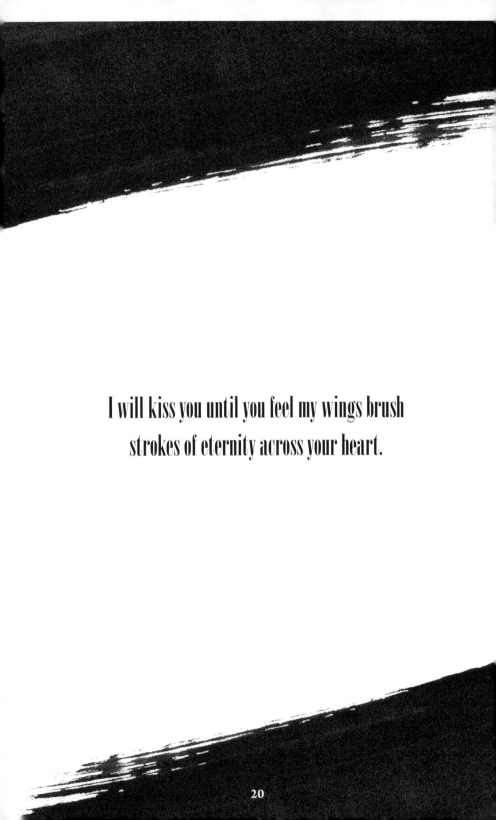

I will kiss you until you feel my wings brush
strokes of eternity across your heart.

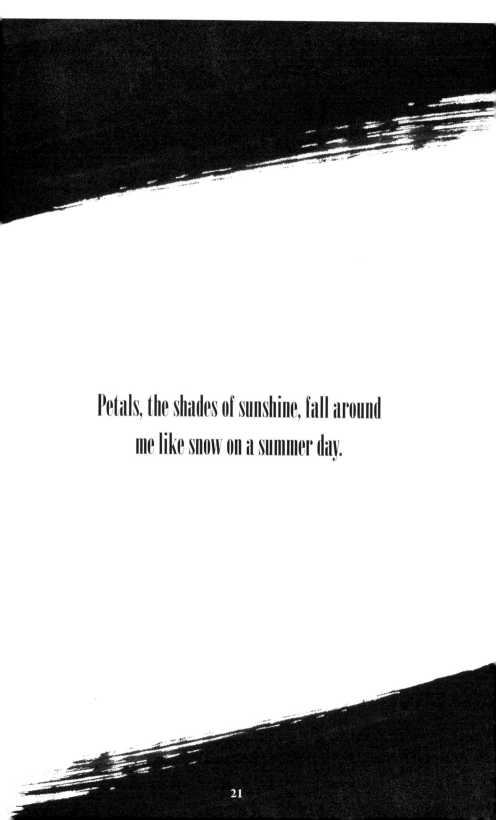

Petals, the shades of sunshine, fall around
me like snow on a summer day.

Join the rain.

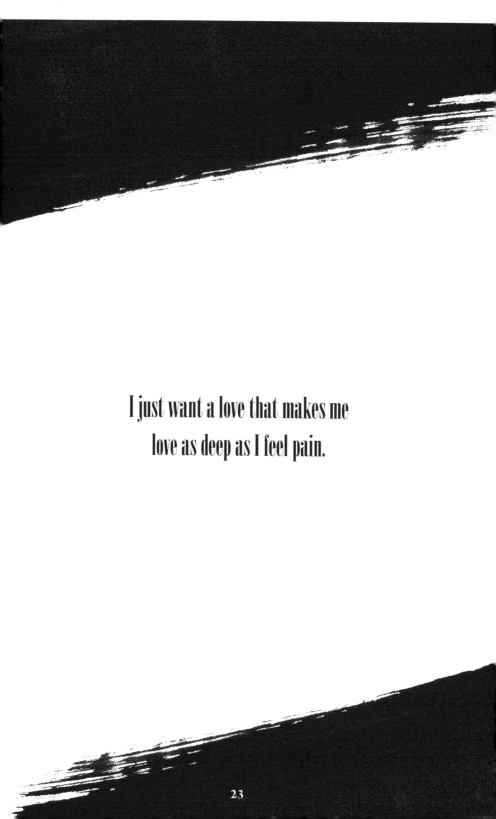

I just want a love that makes me
love as deep as I feel pain.

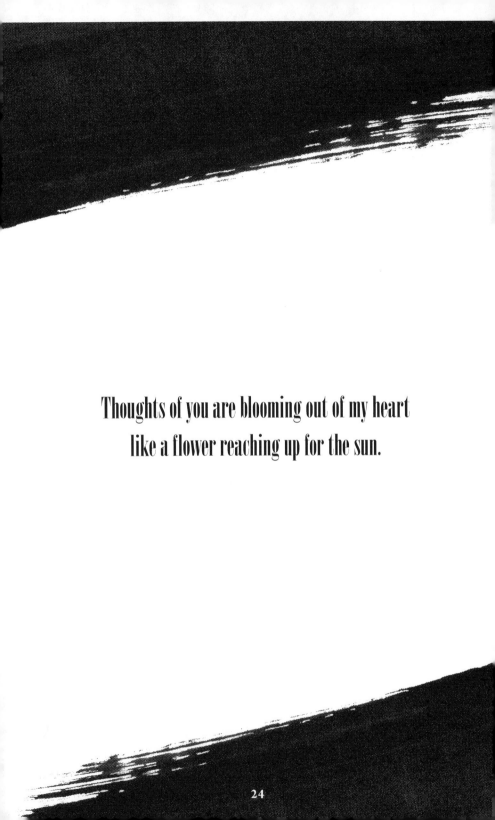

Thoughts of you are blooming out of my heart
like a flower reaching up for the sun.

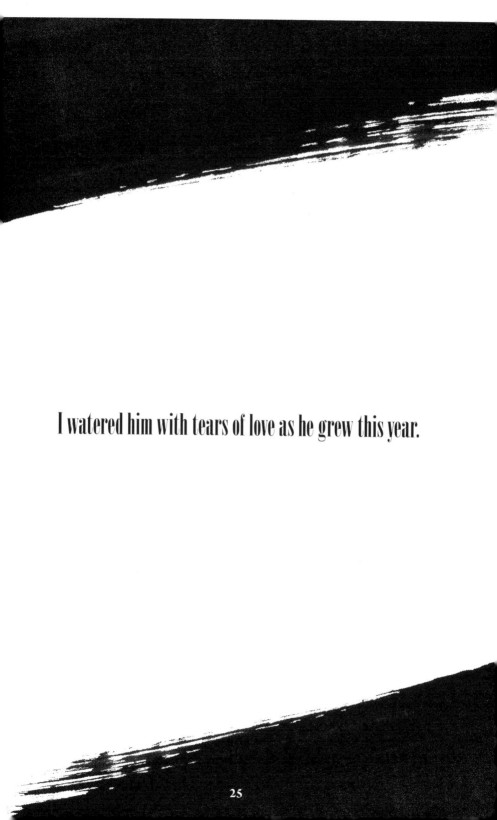

I watered him with tears of love as he grew this year.

When I lay on his skin, I feel his soul.

Love spilled out when you tripped over my heart.

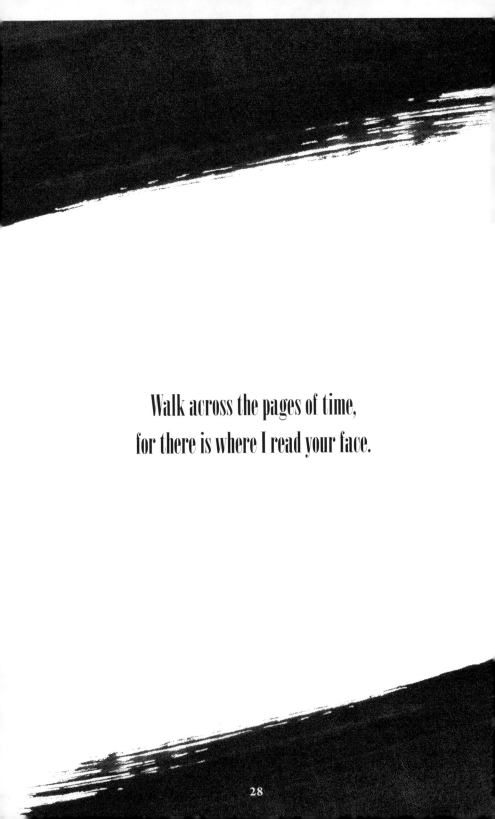

Walk across the pages of time,
for there is where I read your face.

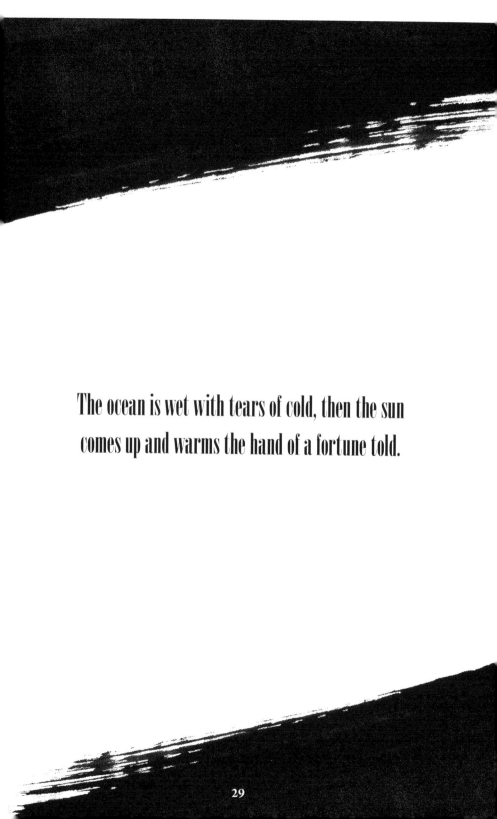

The ocean is wet with tears of cold, then the sun
comes up and warms the hand of a fortune told.

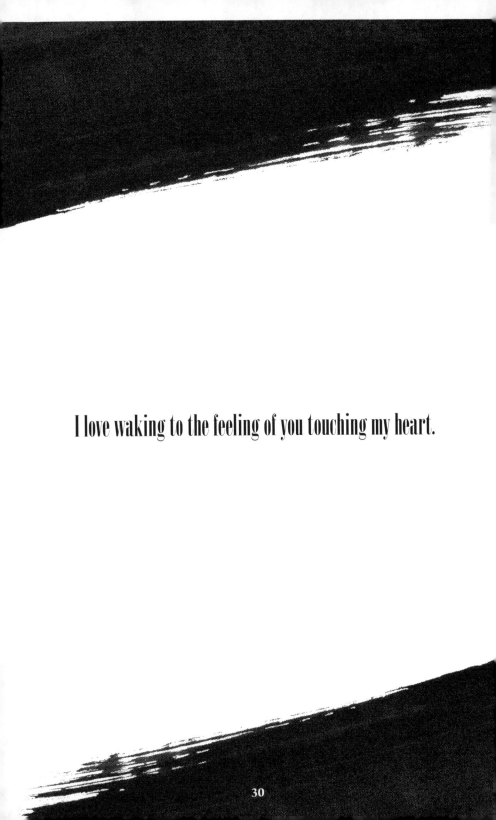

I love waking to the feeling of you touching my heart.

Set him free; locked emotions are twisted within.

I feel you near when you are not.

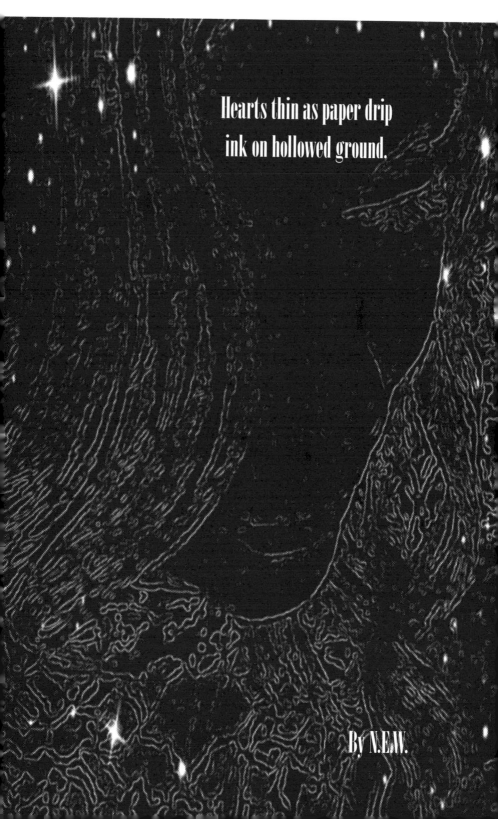

Hearts thin as paper drip
ink on hollowed ground.

By N.E.W.

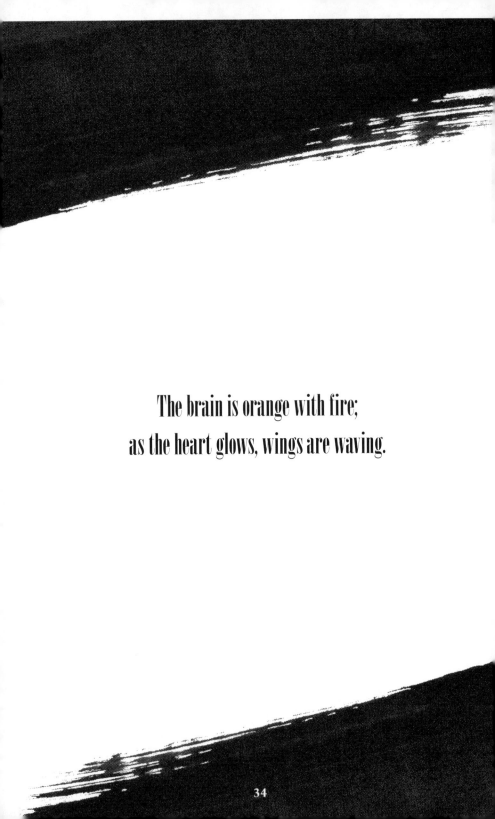

The brain is orange with fire;
as the heart glows, wings are waving.

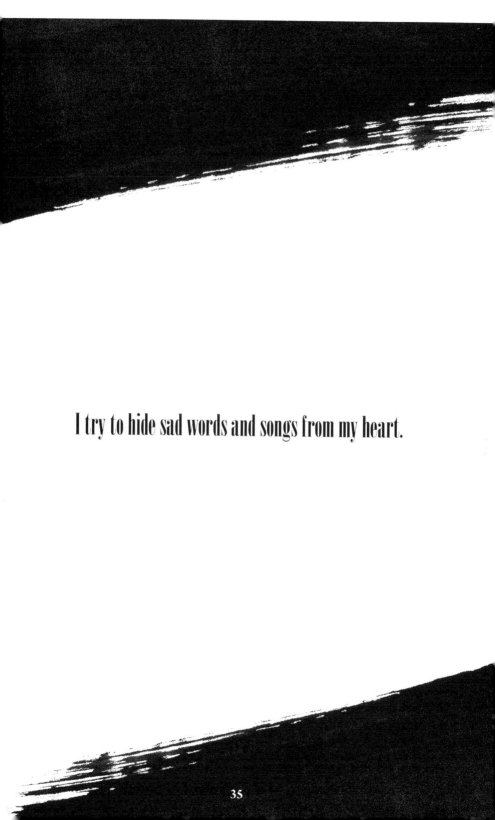

I try to hide sad words and songs from my heart.

Your lips don't move; I feel the words you speak.

There is no time, just moments to be awake.

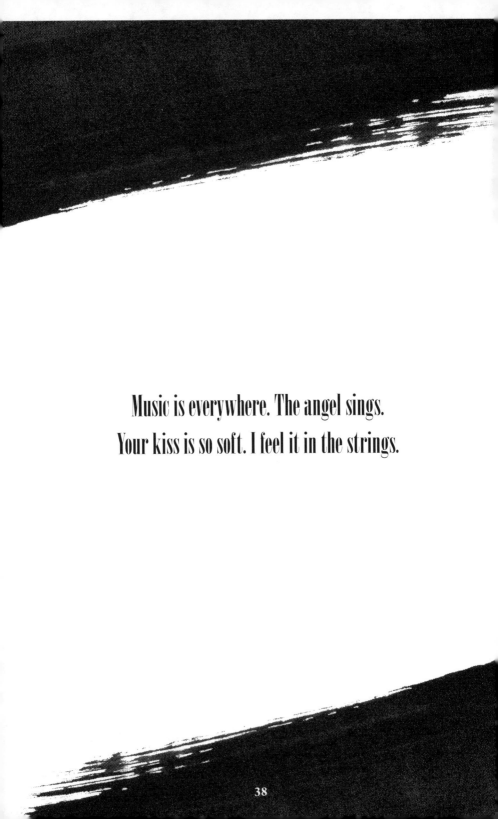

Music is everywhere. The angel sings.
Your kiss is so soft. I feel it in the strings.

Do you feel my heart's soul? It's loving you.

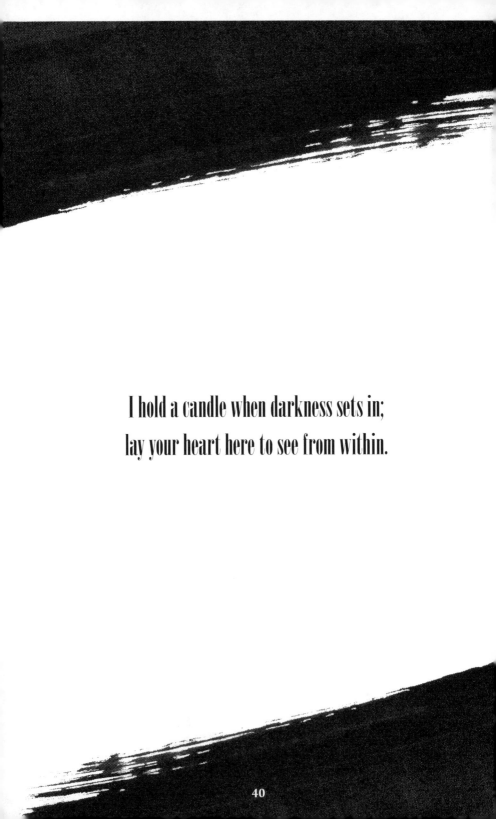

I hold a candle when darkness sets in;
lay your heart here to see from within.

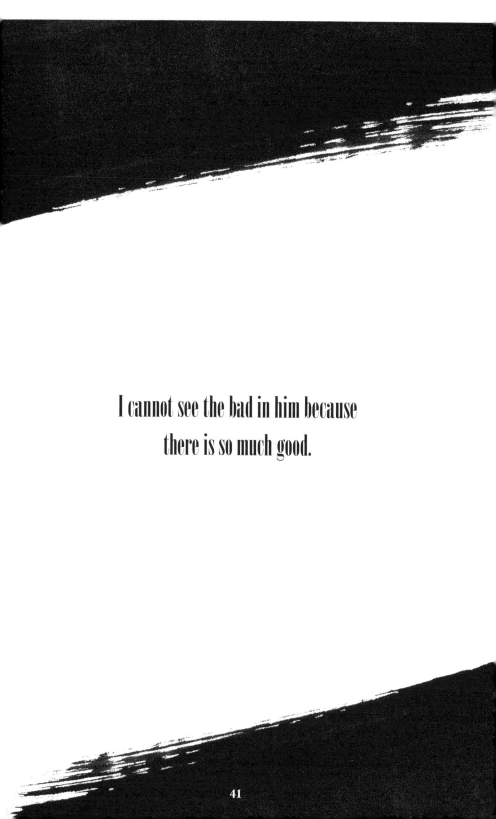

I cannot see the bad in him because
there is so much good.

Your lips are the spark, that starts the
heart to feel your warm embrace.

A tree just sits there and never leaves.

Our hearts grow from one energy spark.

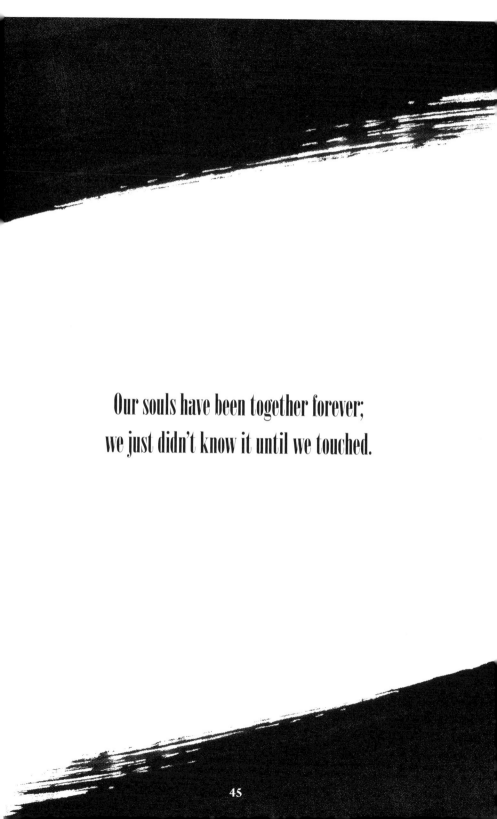

Our souls have been together forever;
we just didn't know it until we touched.

The universe speaks out of love and necessity.

Here the whispers of my soul.

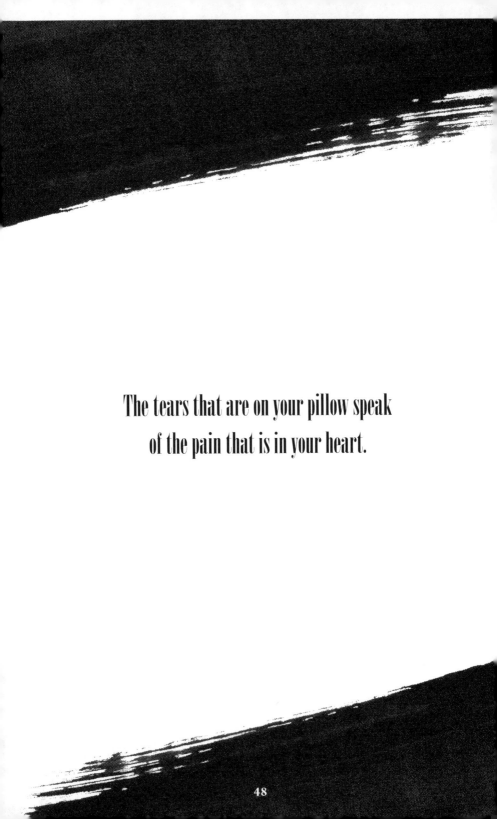

The tears that are on your pillow speak
of the pain that is in your heart.

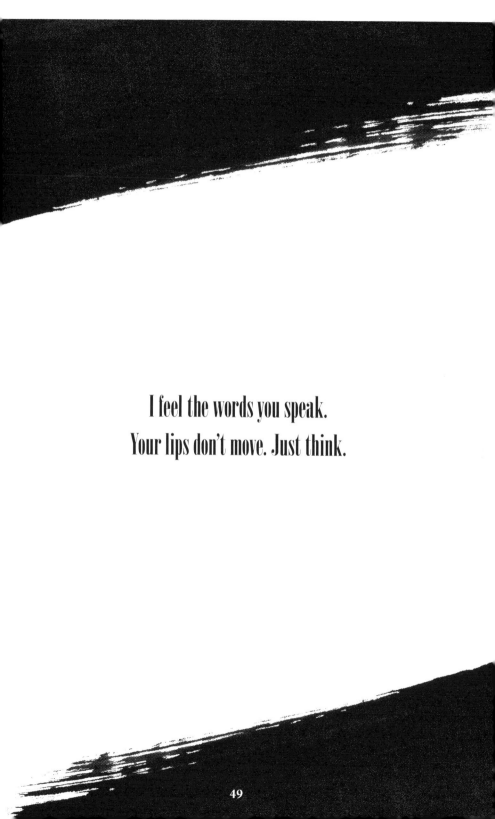

I feel the words you speak.
Your lips don't move. Just think.

Notions of tomorrow are loving guidance sent to you.

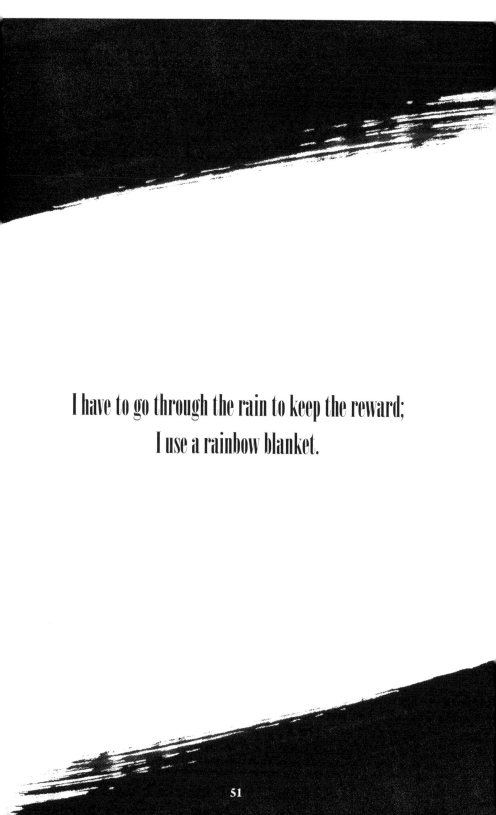

I have to go through the rain to keep the reward;
I use a rainbow blanket.

When I am just being myself, the universe speaks.

You make my us.

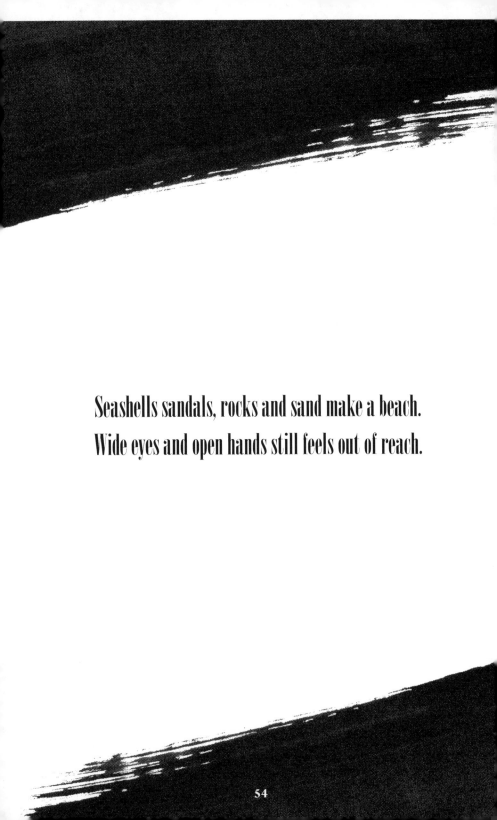

Seashells sandals, rocks and sand make a beach.
Wide eyes and open hands still feels out of reach.

We cannot wrap the truly important gifts.

Tell me a story.

By N.E.W.

Unspoken words hurt your heart.

Being in the state of mystification, a woman receives repetitive messages from an unknown spirit who is beyond the veil of her own reality. As she transitions from her physical reality into her dream world, the messages become so intrusive and disrupting. She must write them down on a piece of paper she keeps next to her bedside to later share them with those for whom they are intended to find. Or is the voice her own higher self, guiding and encouraging her on her road to continuous growth and higher learning?

Journal your thoughts, dreams and experiences

Journal your thoughts, dreams and experiences

Journal your thoughts, dreams and experiences

Journal your thoughts, dreams and experiences

Journal your thoughts, dreams and experiences

Journal your thoughts, dreams and experiences

Journal your thoughts, dreams and experiences

Journal your thoughts, dreams and experiences

Journal your thoughts, dreams and experiences

Journal your thoughts, dreams and experiences

Journal your thoughts, dreams and experiences

Journal your thoughts, dreams and experiences

Journal your thoughts, dreams and experiences

Journal your thoughts, dreams and experiences

Journal your thoughts, dreams and experiences

Journal your thoughts, dreams and experiences

Journal your thoughts, dreams and experiences

Journal your thoughts, dreams and experiences

Journal your thoughts, dreams and experiences

Journal your thoughts, dreams and experiences

_____

_____

_____

_____

_____

_____

_____

_____

_____

_____

_____

_____

_____

_____

_____

_____

_____

_____

_____

_____

_____

_____

_____

_____

_____

Journal your thoughts, dreams and experiences

Journal your thoughts, dreams and experiences

Journal your thoughts, dreams and experiences

Journal your thoughts, dreams and experiences

Journal your thoughts, dreams and experiences

Journal your thoughts, dreams and experiences

Journal your thoughts, dreams and experiences

Journal your thoughts, dreams and experiences

Journal your thoughts, dreams and experiences

Journal your thoughts, dreams and experiences

Journal your thoughts, dreams and experiences

Journal your thoughts, dreams and experiences

Journal your thoughts, dreams and experiences

Journal your thoughts, dreams and experiences

Journal your thoughts, dreams and experiences

Journal your thoughts, dreams and experiences

Journal your thoughts, dreams and experiences

Journal your thoughts, dreams and experiences

Journal your thoughts, dreams and experiences

Printed in the United States
by Baker & Taylor Publisher Services